Self Care
isn't Selfish

YOUR ROADMAP FOR TAKING RESPONSIBILITY
FOR YOUR OWN HAPPINESS

Self Care
Well

Susie Ascott

Copyright

First published by www.bookpod.com.au. For distribution details and how to order please visit www.presentperfect.com.au

ISBN: 978-0-9943633-0-5

Design: Sharon Westin-Shaw - www.sharonwestinshaw.com.au

Editor: Lisa Cropman - www.thewordnest.com.au

Contents

About the Author

Susie Ascott moved into a career as a life coach in 1997 from a background of over 25 years of sales and support services in Information Technology. Her corporate roles have included management, consultancy and project management in the UK and Australia.

The death of her sister from breast cancer at the early age of 50 was the catalyst that gave her the courage to resign from her well-paid corporate role and take the risk of running her own business as a life coach, doing what she really loves.

As an 'on again, off again' yoga student since her early teens she made a commitment to herself to complete a teacher training course and has been teaching and studying Hatha yoga since 2006. Her practices of yoga, permaculture and earth- based spirituality, along with a love of gardening, reading, writing and painting, inform her approach to life coaching.

Susie readily admits that she spent many years believing that self care was selfish. When her second marriage ended in divorce she resolved to stop practicing self neglect and begin the journey to valuing herself and her happiness.

You can find out more about Susie at www.presentperfect. com.au where, amongst other things, she explains in further detail her choice of logo for her business, Present Perfect.

The Vesica Piscis is formed by the intersection of two circles or spheres whose centres exactly touch. I chose the Vesica Piscis to represent my business because this symbolic intersection represents the **common ground, shared vision and mutual understanding between equal individuals**. My intention is to work with you in a true partnership.

The shape of the human eye itself is a Vesica Piscis. The spiritual significance of **seeing eye-to-eye** to the **mirror of the soul** was highly regarded by numerous Renaissance artists who used this form extensively in art and architecture. My aim is to connect with my clients at this level of deep understanding.

Introduction

Have you ever found yourself saying or thinking, 'What about *me*? When do *I* get a go?' and immediately felt guilty? I know I have. I returned to full-time corporate work when my babies were six months old, and I was the sole carer for my own mother when she developed dementia. I understand what it's like to be time poor and feel exhausted and guilty.

If being kind, helpful and caring towards others is a natural part of who you are, but you find it hard to do something kind for yourself, this book is for you.

In my work as a life coach and a yoga teacher, I've worked with many wonderful people who are natural givers. From this experience, and my own personal experiences, I've found that so many of us keep giving and giving without replenishing ourselves. We become more and more exhausted and less and less able to support others. If we don't take action at this point, then we can find ourselves getting exhausted, sick or resentful, and even acting out passive aggressive behaviours.

I've walked alongside clients as they began to embrace the concept of self care and took the steps to becoming responsible for their own happiness. I watched them becoming not only happier within themselves, but also more truly helpful and supportive to others. This is what I want for us all.

This book shows you how to use your skills of kindness and unconditional support to embrace the power of self care. It shows you why and how to value your life and take responsibility for your own happiness. The wonderful outcome is that you will then be in a position to extend even more kindness and care to others, without depleting yourself.

This is a short, practical guide based on straightforward principles and pragmatic suggestions. There are no promises of silver bullets or magical secrets and you don't need to dedicate a lot of time or any money.

First we'll look at selfishness so that we can get this out of the way and understand that looking after ourselves is far from selfish. Then we'll discuss the risks of self neglect. We'll define self care as the act of listening to messages from our mind, body and spirit and responding to them in ways that nourish and replenish us. Although there are underlying themes that are common to us all, exactly what constitutes self care is different for each of us at different times in our lives.

Much of our behaviour is determined by our belief systems and our habits. Belief systems are a mental representation of an attitude and are not necessarily based on evidence. Habits are activities that we do subconsciously and frequently. Both belief systems and habits can be supportive or unhelpful and they are not set in stone, we can change them if we want to. We'll consider what changes you might choose to make to your beliefs and habits, and how this is done. To help you explore new ideas and behaviours, we'll use the analogy of a road map. The map is complete with locations, signposts, road hazards and pathways that guide you to recognise what it is that **you** need - and how to make that happen. In the final chapters we'll identify where you are on the map, and you'll begin to make lasting changes for your stress-free journey to happiness.

It is my intention that this book gives you:

- The understanding and acceptance that self care is vital if you are to fully embody the kind and caring person you truly are.
- A roadmap to guide you as you journey towards a happier more fulfilling life.
- Encouragement, as you take practical steps to embrace the power of self care, now.

As with all guide books and maps, I suggest that you read through the book once to get a feel for the landscape - the locations, signposts, road hazards and principles of how to navigate, then work through it again completing the exercises. I hope you will keep the book handy and refer back to it often.

May you enjoy this exciting and rewarding experience. I look forward to sharing it with you.

> 'The best effect of any book is that it
> excites the reader to self activity.'
>
> Thomas Carlyle, philosopher and essayist

Chapter One
On selfishness and self care

The human traits of kindness and caring are wonderful attributes and, if you're reading this book, I'm pretty sure that it's natural for you to care about, and for, others. For many of us, being kind and caring towards ourselves is a lot less natural. We've been led to believe that looking after ourselves is selfish. A quick search online brings up the following definition:

Selfish

adjective

- chiefly concerned with one's own interest, advantage, etc., esp to the total exclusion of the interests of others

- a selfish person is a disagreeable person, unpleasant person, egocentric, egoist, exploiter, user, hog, pig

No wonder we find it hard to practice self care if we believe that self care is going to turn us into an egocentric exploiter.

Many Christian-based western religions tend to emphasise caring for others and, if we look to the East, we see that Buddhism emphasises compassion practices. These teachings can get into our psyche and reinforce our fear of becoming selfish. However, it is important to note that

Christianity, Buddhism and the science of psychology recognise that self-compassion is a precursor to compassion for others.

From my personal experience and through working with clients who, like you, are naturally kind and caring, I want to reassure you that those who practice self care are far from selfish. Self care is simply about taking responsibility for your own happiness and wellbeing. The outcome is that you then have energy available to provide support for others. Intellectually, this probably seems obvious. 'I know that!' I hear you say, and then I hear a *but* - '*but* I don't have the time', '*but* the children need me', '*but* it's so HARD', '*but* [fill in your own excuse here]'.

I understand, and I've been there. The good news is that we can all make some changes and even small changes can produce immediate tangible benefits.

Self neglect

Take a deep breath; some uncomfortable truths are coming up. The opposite of self care is self neglect. Self neglect can easily and surreptitiously lead us into dangerous ground. Not looking after ourselves properly results in unintended outcomes, and the complete opposite of our original intention to show kindness to others. Whilst it's important to care about, and for, others, there are huge risks if we go over the top and always put our own needs last.

We can become *exhausted or ill*. Not only are we then unable to help anyone else, we become the ones who need help from others. As the flight attendants remind us, we need to put on our own oxygen mask first before we can help others.

We can become *resentful or bitter* and no one wants to be around someone in this state of mind and heart. Let's face it, we don't even want to be around ourselves when we feel like this. But, hang on a minute, don't beat yourself up about this. Resentment is telling us something important. We'll discuss this further in later chapters. For now, please resist the temptation to feel guilty.

In an attempt to get our loved ones to notice how much we are doing for them, we can find ourselves behaving in rather desperate ways. We might make a lot of noise washing the dishes as our partner lies on the couch watching TV, or we might make a big deal of getting the children to pick their feet up so we can vacuum under them as they sit with eyes glued to their iPhone. We want them to notice how hard we're working in the hope that this will stir them into offering to help. Of course, it doesn't work and, OMG, are we actually becoming *passive-aggressive* or even approaching full-on *martyrdom?*

We can eventually *reach the end of our tether* and swing to the other end of the spectrum, suddenly walking out on a marriage or quitting our job, for example, leaving those around us, and ourselves, confused and hurt.

If we are aware of these feelings and we look them in the eye, we can take them for what they are. They are purely signposts, messages that we are giving away more than we have available right now. These signs don't mean you're a bad person, they just indicate that you are, currently, not in a good place.

So, we don't want to be selfish and we don't want to neglect our own needs. We need to be in balance, being both kind and helpful to others and practicing self care.

'There is no one in the universe more dear to us than ourselves. The mind may travel in a thousand directions, but it will find no one else more beloved. The moment you see how important it is to love yourself, you will stop making others suffer.

Thich Nhat Hanh, spiritual leader

Self care

Self care is taking responsibility for our own happiness and wellbeing. Through this practice we keep our energy levels topped up. The outcomes are:

- We don't become a burden to others.
- We are vibrant and inspiring.
- We are good to be around.
- We are a better friend.

- We enjoy life more.
- We are able to follow our natural instincts to support and care for and about others, with a big smile on our face and in our heart.

Exactly what we do to practice self care will be different for each one of us. The principles, however, are the same for us all - we need to:

- Let go of some of the things which drain us, and add in more things that nourish us.
- Be realistic about what we have control over and what is outside of our control.
- Assess what resources we have available, such as time, money and people who can help.
- Make changes at a pace which works for us.

In some instances, all we can change is our thoughts, and sometimes this is all that is needed. Usually, we can make some small changes and often we can make bigger changes. The more we practice the better we feel and the easier it gets. Most of us slip back at times, but each time we do, we can pick ourselves up more quickly and slip back less frequently.

I would like you to consider self care as a practice rather than a goal because a practice is something we can easily continue throughout our life. Goals, such as running a marathon, have a definite end point. When it comes to self care, we are not trying to get somewhere and then stop and say, 'Yay! Done it!' We are aiming to make small and big changes to our everyday ways of being in the world. This is an ongoing journey where every step brings immediate benefits. The more you practice the easier it becomes, until it is just a natural way of being, a part of who you are.

So, are you ready to move on to practice self care? You have the skills already. You know how to be a good friend, non-judgmental, kind, caring and sensitive to other people's needs. You know how to give unconditional support and encouragement. It's time to practice treating yourself this way.

Lessons from Chapter One

Self care is not selfish - it is taking responsibility for my own happiness.

Self care is an important part of my life - it gives me the energy and nourishment I need to achieve great things. It is the basis for my wellbeing.

Self neglect makes me vulnerable to selfish behaviour - I can use my existing skills to be kind to myself.

Self care is an ongoing practice - I shall eliminate, reduce, or change my attitude to the activities that drain me. I shall add in activities that nourish me.

GO ROUND AGAIN CIRCUIT

RESENTMENT ROAD

DEPRESSION SWAMP

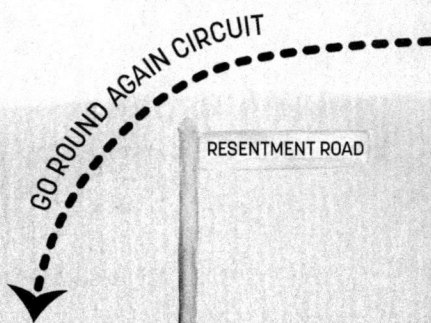

EXHAUSTION HOLLOW

ASKING FOR HELP ROCKFACE

YOU ARE NOW IN
THE SHIRE
OF SHOULD

PASSIVE AGGRESSIVE TRAP

MARTYR MOUNTAIN RANGE

ANGER VOLCANO

BEATING YOURSELF UP
BUSHLAND

THE
HEARTLANDS

Chapter Two
The map

The art of self care requires listening and responding to the messages from your mind, body and spirit. We're going to explore this with the aid of a map. The map represents our journey. By reading the signs on the map we can discover where we are, and, more importantly, what direction to take in order to find our way to a better place.

The signposts

Just like those on a map, the signs we come across in life are messages we must pay attention to. They come in the three forms:

- *Emotions* - such as resentment, anger, frustration and irritability.
- *Physical symptoms* - such as headaches, lethargy, sleeplessness, aches and pains.
- *Spiritually* - in the form of hopelessness, despair or depression.

What I want for you is to be especially mindful that these messages of mind, body and spirit do not mean you are a bad person. They are valuable signs that alert you to the fact that you're giving away more energy than you are taking in, your fuel tank is running low and it's time to top it up.

When's the last time you took the time to address the feelings that are asking for your attention?

Once you notice a sign, it's time to pause and ask yourself some questions. Your internal conversation might look something like this:

I feel scattered and agitated. *What is this showing me?*

That I feel overwhelmed. *Why am I overwhelmed?*

I'm spending time on something that really doesn't feel important to me; it looks like I have my priorities wrong.

What do I need to do?

I need to remind myself of what's important to me and let go of the rest.

What do I need right now?

I need to be alone for five minutes and ground myself. Then I need to go through my diary and do some serious rescheduling.

'Asking the proper question is the central action of transformation – in fairy tales, in analysis, and in individuation. The key question causes germination of consciousness. The properly shaped question always emanates from an essential curiosity about what stands behind. Questions are the keys that cause the secret doors of the psyche to swing open.'

Clarissa Pinkola Estés, author

The locations

All around the map are Self Care Wells, places where you can stop for a moment or stop for a day or more and top up your energy and happiness. Exactly what we choose to draw from the Self Care Wells will be different for each of us.

Most of the area on the map is within The Heartlands. Here, you are balancing self care with care for others. You are getting pleasure and energy from looking after yourself and have plenty of energy to share with others in ways that nourish you and them.

Outside of The Heartlands is the Land of Self Neglect. We are going to take a closer look at the locations within the Land of Self Neglect.

Exhaustion Hollow

The signs you're nearing or have come to Exhaustion Hollow are straightforward enough. You might feel:

- physically exhausted
- mentally overwhelmed
- spiritually weary
- all of the above.

What to do if you reach Exhaustion Hollow?

The principle, at each of the locations in the Land of Self

Neglect is to pause, breathe in and out, and ask yourself some questions. The first question to ask is, 'Can I make the time right now to have this conversation with myself and consider what I need to do?' If the baby is screaming, for example, or there's no way you can stop right now, perhaps all you can do in the moment is breathe in and out again.

> 'Sometimes the most important thing
> in a whole day is the rest we take
> between two deep breaths.'
>
> Etty Hillesum, letter writer and diarist (1914-1943)

As soon as the crisis is over you need to take some nourishment from one of your Self Care Wells. To decide what you need, have your conversation with yourself. If you are physically exhausted, do you need rest? Do you need something to eat? If you are mentally overwhelmed perhaps you need to go for a run? Are you spiritually weary, feeling down and flat? Would a walk in nature help? There is no one-size-fits-all answer, but using your intuition and through experimenting you will soon learn what it is you need.

Lou, a client and the mother of a toddler, uses the following flow-chart:

I have a mental flow chart that I try to refer to when I'm crabby:

Step 1: Am I hungry? (Y) have a snack (N) - refer to step 2

Step 2: Do I need a nap? (Y) take a nap (N) - proceed with crabbiness enquiry

Warning! If you don't take action, but keep going on this path you will meet a fork in the road that leads to either Depression Swamp or Resentment Road.

Depression Swamp

In Depression Swamp you might feel:

- grey
- numb
- everything is too much effort
- no joy
- no motivation
- shame or guilt
- a fragile sense of self-worth.

This, like Eyeore's home in *Winnie the Pooh*, is a sad and boggy place.

Note: we are talking, here, about situational depression. It is a temporary, manageable feeling and you are able to know why you are feeling depressed. If it's an ongoing feeling and you can't find a cause, then do consider getting help from a healthcare professional.

What to do if you reach Depression Swamp?

Pause, take a breath in and out, and ask yourself some questions. Remember you got here via Exhaustion Hollow, so check out the questions above. Do you need physical rest or food? Do you need some mental stimulation, some spiritual nourishment? What small things can you do for yourself to give yourself energy? Do you need company? Do you need to be alone? What if you put on some favourite music and danced wildly?

'I just finished a nightmare of a group assignment that involved way too much caffeine, lack of sleep, etc. I think I went past my threshold and feel a bit damaged right now – to the point of not being quite emotionally healthy. But it's a good lesson in noticing how so many of my unhelpful thought patterns and cycles arise from poor health and habits and lack of listening to one's body. No wonder I used to get depressed so easily.' … 'Will be taking a deep break today to heal my mind, then cheerfully continue with the (next) assignment I have already started.'

M. life coaching client, Melbourne

Resentment Road

If you find yourself becoming resentful, you are probably on Resentment Road. This leads towards the Passive Aggressive Trap and, from there, the ranges of Martyr Mountain can be seen on the horizon. The positive aspect of Resentment Road is that resentment itself is a form of energy. It's not a healthy energy, but you can transform it into something positive.

As we travel along Resentment Road we find ourselves:

- Giving without joy.

- Struggling to get acknowledgement or thanks for all that we are doing.
- Feeling unappreciated.

What to do if you reach Resentment Road?

Pause, take a breath in and out. Ask yourself some questions. Specifically, 'Why am I not being appreciated?' We have been taught, 'Do unto others as you would have them do unto you.' In a general sense this is good advice - we want to treat others with respect, with compassion and without judgement. However, if what you are giving is not being appreciated, then I suggest you consider another way of looking at things. 'Do unto others as *they* would have you do unto *them*.'

The signpost alerts us to two important possibilities:

- Maybe what you're giving is something you need to either do for yourself, or ask others to do for you, i.e. 'Do unto others as you would have them do unto you'.

Alternatively:

- Perhaps what you're giving is not what the recipient wants, i.e. 'Do unto others as *they* would have you do unto *them*'.

Much as many of us might develop an intuition or awareness of what others are wanting, feeling or thinking, we still need to communicate clearly. Phrases such as 'But he should know what I want,' and 'She should appreciate all that I am doing for her,' are not helpful if they don't know or don't appreciate. It doesn't necessarily mean that they don't care about you. After all, you are giving (and giving) what you think they want, because you do care. Maybe what you're giving just isn't what they want.

> 'The single biggest problem
> in communication is the illusion
> that it has taken place.'
>
> George Bernard Shaw, playwright

Your conversation with yourself needs to cover:

- What is it that I need to do for myself?
- What is it that I need to ask for?

And then, perhaps:

- What is it that I could give instead, that will be appreciated?

Passive Aggressive Trap

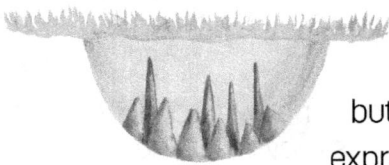

In the Passive Aggressive Trap we are feeling angry, but we have been taught not to express our anger; to express anger puts us at risk of being rejected or criticised. To protect our self-imposed need for acceptance we manifest our repressed emotions through passive aggressive behaviours such as:

- sullenness
- stubbornness
- giving the silent treatment
- being sarcastic, rolling our eyes and saying 'of course nothing's wrong'.

What to do if you reach Passive Aggressive Trap?

Remember that this behaviour stems from a desire to please other people; a desire to avoid conflict and keep everyone happy. It's just that you have forgotten that you also have the right to express your own wants and needs. By making yourself a priority you can learn that you can get your needs met by openly expressing your feelings calmly and communicating clearly.

'Being direct is less confusing and allows for a stimulating dialogue rather than frustrating disconnections.'
Susan Solomon, psychotherapist

Martyr Mountain Range

When you reach Martyr Mountain Range you may find yourself tempted to sacrifice even more of yourself for the sake of others. You may

feel that to do any less than you are, would be acting selfishly. Perhaps you are actively seeking thanks and acknowledgement through complaining and pointing out to others all that you do for them. This need for thanks and acknowledgement is a substitute for what you really need. You need some nourishment from your Self Care Wells.

What to do if you reach Martyr Mountain Range?

Pause, take several breaths in and out. Don't despair and please don't beat yourself up if you start to notice the signs. Have your conversation with yourself. Maybe it's time to ask clearly for some help. When you are in Martyr Mountain Range it is difficult to accept the help of others. Difficult and uncomfortable, yes, but you can do it. A sense of humour, a sense of self compassion and a trust in your ability to make changes to your belief systems and behaviours will all help you to turn around and stride purposefully back to the Heartlands.

'From what I've seen, it isn't so much the act of asking that paralyses us - it's what lies beneath: the fear of being vulnerable, the fear of rejection, the fear of looking needy or weak. The fear of being seen as a burdensome member of the community instead of a productive one.'

Amanda Palmer, author

The Shire of Should

The signs that you are in The Shire of Should are many and varied and may include any, or all, of the messages we have been discussing above: resentment, exhaustion, overwhelm, frustration. Shame and guilt may be lurking around.

Here, we are expending energy on activities or concerns for no reason other than somewhere along our journey we have taken on board someone else's values. We are doing things merely because we feel we should. Perhaps you feel you should keep the house spotlessly clean and tidy. Maybe you think you should give 110% effort to everything you do? You should attempt to climb the corporate ladder? Perhaps you are an excellent cook and feel you should produce a gourmet meal whenever you have friends or family over for dinner.

What to do if you reach The Shire of Should?

Pause, take a breath in and out. Ask yourself some questions. It's tempting to ask yourself where these belief systems come from; who, or what, has caused you to feel you should? Why have you taken on these values which are not your own? This might be a helpful line of enquiry. You may, however, find it more helpful to simply ask yourself, 'What are the benefits of continuing to spend time on this activity?' and 'What are the benefits of no longer doing it?' Consider the truth: - you don't have to do something just because you are good at it.

> 'To be yourself in a world that is constantly trying to make you something else is the greatest accomplishment.'
>
> Ralph Waldo Emerson, essayist and poet

Well-Worn Pathways

Leading towards all these locations there will be Well-Worn Pathways, paths we travel from habit or outdated belief systems.

There may be some things which take up your time and energy that were necessary when you first started them but are now no longer necessary or helpful. For example, packing school lunches may have been a requirement when the children were younger, but do they still need you to do it for them now they are 14?

We are creatures of habit and we can use this weakness as a strength, as we build new habits and take on new belief systems.

The Baggage of Shame

Shame and feelings of inadequacy or unworthiness deserve a separate mention. Rather than lurking around specific locations, I consider these to be the unnecessary luggage we carry around with us, like heavy backpacks. We all have these feelings from time to time. For some of us they can be constant companions weighing us down and stopping us from travelling back to The Heartlands.

I have found Brené Brown's research and writing on shame to be extremely helpful (see Resources). In her research she found a correlation between perfectionism and shame. Her research also suggests that shame is at the root of narcissism. This unsettling finding indicates that narcissism is another risk of spending too long in the Land of Self Neglect. To help us become more resilient to the Shame Gremlins, Brené Brown recommends practicing creative pursuits and trying out new activities where we can give ourselves permission to be a beginner and have correspondingly low expectations of our performance and outcomes. I think of this as practicing doing things wholeheartedly, rather than doing them perfectly.

> 'Lighten up on yourself. No one is perfect. Gently accept your humanness.'
>
> Deborah Day, psychologist

The Heartlands

Before we all get too upset and depressed thinking about these locations in the Land of Self Neglect, let's remind ourselves that most of the land available to us is within The Heartlands. Here is where we'll learn to

stay for as much of our life as we can. As we get more and more practiced at looking after ourselves, The Heartlands expand and the Land of Self Neglect gets pushed further and further away.

Pathways back to The Heartlands

Working through the next chapters, you will begin to build some new pathways back into to The Heartlands. You can walk them at your own pace, erecting your own signposts to follow and installing your own Self Care Wells to nourish you.

Lessons from Chapter Two

Self care is an ongoing practice.

I will take the time to listen to the messages from my mind, body and spirit.

These messages come in the form of emotions and mental, physical and spiritual symptoms.

I will pause and have a conversation with myself whenever I feel less than okay and take some nourishment from a Self Care Well.

I will question myself to discover what I can change in my behaviour, thoughts and belief systems.

Chapter Three
Road hazards along the way

As you begin to clear some new pathways back to The Heartlands, you'll most likely encounter some road hazards along the way. If you know about them you'll be able to navigate them and take them in your stride.

Depending on the particular road hazards that block your path, you may also find it helpful to work with a relevant professional, such as a food coach, a health professional, a personal trainer, or a life coach who can help you make changes.

> 'Asking for help does not mean that we are weak or incompetent. It usually indicates an advanced level of honesty and intelligence.'
> Anne Wilson Schaef, author

The following road hazards are the most common that clients and I have experienced, and this is how we've navigated them with kindness and a smile.

Beating Yourself Up Bushlands

We've talked about Well-Worn Pathways in the previous chapter. These are our habits, the things we do subconsciously. It's very likely that despite your best efforts and intentions there will be times when you find yourself slipping back into these unsupportive habits. Whilst it's important to stay aware and awake as you build your new pathways, it's equally as important to treat yourself with compassion when you don't. Remember to be kind to yourself as you travel.

> 'Oh the irony of having to be kind to yourself as you learn to be kind to yourself.'
>
> Susie Ascott

So, when you stumble and start berating yourself for lack of willpower, just stop for a few moments and give yourself some self-kindness before recommitting to the journey. Give yourself a metaphorical or literal hug. Visit a Self Care Well.

> 'Be gentle with yourself. You are a child of the universe, no less than the trees and the stars. In the noisy confusion of life, keep peace in your soul.'
>
> Max Ehrmann, writer and poet

Remember that you have been putting yourself last, perhaps for many years, so attempting to change your habits and beliefs will also take time. Don't expect to change radically overnight.

> 'All great achievements require time.'
> Maya Angelou, author

Example #1: Beating Yourself Up Bushlands

Let's imagine that you decide you're going to practice saying no to unrealistic requests for help from your work colleague. Your colleague comes to you in tears at 5pm and asks you to proofread their report in time for an 8am meeting the next day. You find yourself agreeing to take it home with you. You cancel your plans for the evening, spending your time re-writing their report for them. This is when you might start talking to yourself unkindly with phrases like, 'You *never* have any will power', 'What's the point of trying to change?', 'You're *always* going to be a hopeless case,. I encourage you to stop beating yourself up as soon as you notice yourself doing it. Notice whether shame or guilty feelings are showing up. Be kind to yourself and give yourself some encouragement to keep trying. Resolve to talk with yourself as you would to a good friend. Once you have given yourself your metaphorical or literal hug, then you can consider what you might be able to do differently next time. How can you make it easier to say no? Perhaps you could write your appointments with yourself in ink in your diary: Appointment with Self, 7pm-9pm (yoga class). The next time your colleague asks you to do something unreasonable, you can graciously say, 'No, I can't, I have a prior commitment', or 'My diary is full this evening. You're good at your job, I'm sure you can manage it'. Practice a few phrases in front of a mirror until you're comfortable with them. It may help if you resist the temptation to use the words 'I'm sorry'. You may feel sorry for your colleague that they believe they need your help; but try not to sound apologetic for your considered choices.

Remember to be your own best friend. You might like to write a big sign and put it up on the mirror.

Would you talk to your best friend the way you sometimes talk to yourself?

Asking for Help Rock Face

Most of us have resistance to change. When a business runs a project to implement a new process or system, its success or failure is dependent on the quality of its change management skills and processes. Everyone involved needs to be comfortable with, and supportive of, the new system. So, as well as being aware of our own resistance

to change, we need to be aware that those around us are likely to feel uncomfortable and confused as they see us changing. Friends and family, who truly love and care about you, may seem to be acting in non-supportive ways. You will most likely feel pressure from them to give up your efforts to change and return to your old habits. Feelings of guilt or shame may surface, and you may wonder if you are being selfish. You might feel unloved and unsupported.

Understand that your friends and family do not intend to be unkind; they are uncomfortable, and they are confused. They just need you to let them know what's happening. It's important to let those around you know that you still love and care for them and that you're changing your habits to include looking after your own needs as well as the needs of others. If you have been doing a lot for them, they're going to have to change too, maybe step up and start doing more for themselves. If you want them to come on the journey with you, they need information and time to make changes, too. The conversations you have, how you have them, and with whom, will vary, but we do need to gently bring our family, friends and colleagues along with us.

It may feel very unfamiliar and possibly challenging to ask for help and support from others. Once you ask, I believe you will be pleasantly surprised by their eagerness to support you. Remember how you feel when you are in The Heartlands and able to support someone you love. You are being kind if you give your friends and loved ones the opportunity to support you. If they offer support and you turn it down, isn't this like refusing to accept a gift?

Be prepared to ask for what you want. Before making changes, check that you have your support team on board.

'A little boy was having difficulty lifting a heavy stone. His father came along just then. Noting the boy's failure, he asked, "Are you using all your strength?" "Yes, I am," the little boy said impatiently. "No, you are not," the father answered. "I am right here just waiting, and you haven't asked me to help you."'

Anon

Anger Volcano – leading to – Go Round Again Circuit

As we start to understand that self care isn't selfish, anger directed towards ourselves because we didn't realise this earlier, or anger and resentment towards others, can bubble up to the surface. This is when we might react impulsively, fuelled by negative emotions. We can surprise ourselves, and others, by suddenly walking out of our job or ending a relationship, for example. Behind us, and within us, we leave a trail of confusion and exhaustion.

If you have these feelings, take some breaths, take some time and move one baby step at a time. It is possible that you may make some very big changes at some point in the near or distant future. For now, take one step at a time and make changes in yourself, before changing external circumstances. When we react impulsively, we are likely to recreate the same set of circumstances again. It might be a different partner, a different job, or a different environment, but we will encounter the same issues. It's important that you have your new practice of self care firmly under your belt before you make big changes. It's better to stride happily and confidently towards something rather than run stressed and screaming away from something else.

'Very often a change of self is needed more than a change of scene.'

A. C. Benson, author

Lessons from Chapter Three

It's okay to stumble occasionally, to forgive myself and pick myself up.

It's important and kind to ask for what I want and accept the help of my support team.

I shall talk to myself in the way I would talk to my best friend.

It's better to stride happily and confidently towards something rather than run stressed and screaming away from something else.

I shall practice patience and take one step at a time.

Chapter Four

Locating yourself on the map and responding to your signs

Throughout our life, and even throughout each day, we will wander all around the map and this is natural. We want to ensure that we spend as little time as possible outside of The Heartlands in the Land of Self-Neglect.

In theory, it's fairly easy to know when you wander off into the Land of Self-Neglect. However, if you have habitually spent a lot of time neglecting yourself, you are probably used to ignoring the feelings as they just seem normal. What I want for you is that you can get in touch with your feelings more easily, recognise and respond to the signposts more quickly and take action straight away.

In the previous chapters we explored the need, and the process, for listening to your feelings in the moment. Now we are going to dedicate a bit of time to practice this skill in a reflective way. You can review where you are on your journey and start planning some changes. So, when you are ready, let's take a look at:

- What you are doing that's draining you of energy.
- What possibilities are available to you to change, reduce or eliminate them.
- What commitments you are ready to make.

Reader activity #1: Identifying your energy drains

Find a sheet of paper and title it, 'What drains me? What am I doing that leaves me feeling depleted?' If you prefer, you can use worksheet A1 in the Resources section at the back of this book. To help you, here's a list of some of the energy drains that my clients have identified:

- Cleaning up after others.
- Spending time with people who drain me.
- Worrying about others, finances, future, past, just plain worrying.
- Staying late at the office or bringing work home.
- Taking on too much responsibility for others who are quite capable of looking after themselves.
- Doing other people's planning and organising, and how ironic it is that the more we do other people's worrying or planning for them the less appreciative they seem to be.
- Being a parent of babies or small children.
- Caring for a sick or elderly relative.
- Doing things because we think we 'should'.

I imagine you'll be able to think of several things to put on your list right now. Or, maybe you can start the list now and add to it as you go about your activities during the next few days.

There might be some things on your list that you think, No, surely *that* isn't draining my energy? Leave it there anyway and sit with it for a bit. Some of us are natural empaths. Recent research is suggesting that up to 20% of us are hyper-sensitive. This might mean, for example, that being under fluorescent lights for too long, or spending too much time in the company of others, no matter how much we like them, can leave us feeling exhausted. So, if there's something on your list that feels a little weird, don't dismiss it. If it drains you then it drains you; there is no need for judgement.

There might also be something on your list that is a form of self-soothing or self-medication, maybe drinking coffee or a glass (or more) of wine or eating chocolate. This might work in the short-term but ultimately leaves you drained or cranky. Once again, leave it on your list and let go of judgement.

Here's an example list of identified energy drains

Self care isn't selfish

Worksheet A1: Identifying my energy drains (What drains me?)

Ask yourself the questions below and then write a brief description of each activity or situation and its consequence on your energy levels.

- Where am I over-extending my time and energy?

- What signs of self-neglect are showing up?

I'm spending time listening to my work colleague's personal problems. This makes me feel **depleted** and **frustrated** because they don't take my advice and don't seem to want to resolve anything, just complain. It means I have to bring work home at night in order to keep up with my deadlines.

I'm the sole carer for my mother who has dementia - this brings up **sadness and exhaustion and guilt (when I lose patience).**

I worry about finances - this brings up **fear**; I find it really hard to spend money on myself - this brings up **resentment.**

I drink coffee to keep me going to meet a deadline or get through everything on my do list - this eventually results in me feeling too **wired up** to relax.

When I do get some time for myself, I feel too **unmotivated** to do anything much and end up wasting time on the internet or falling asleep in front of the TV. I feel **guilty and annoyed with myself.**

I often find myself volunteering to help out and end up doing more than my fair share of the work. I'm usually the one who ends up taking all the girls to their soccer games every week. This brings up **resentment** and **exhaustion.**

I have two small children and find it very hard to find any time for myself. I often feel **exhausted.**

Looking through your list you'll probably find some things which you feel confident that you can stop doing, some things which you feel you can reduce or modify, some which seem daunting or scary to change and probably some which you truly do wish to continue.

Unless you have a small list and you feel a sense of lightness as you read through it, then it's unrealistic to expect yourself to address them all immediately.

Take a break, give yourself some acknowledgement and, when you're ready, we'll move on to the next step of exploring further.

Reader activity #2: Exploring your energy drains

The Pareto principle, more commonly referred to as the 80/20 rule, is an observation that putting a certain amount of effort into one activity may give you much larger benefits than putting the same amount of effort into a different activity. Let's use this principle and identify which energy drains you could change that would give you the biggest benefit for the least amount of difficulty and effort. For each of the items on your list, ask yourself the following questions:

- How hard does it feel to let go of this?
- How would I feel better if I let it go?

Now, complete worksheet A2 for each of your energy drains.

Note: There are four blank A2 worksheets in the Resource section in which you can explore your energy drains. For more blank A2 worksheets, email me at susie_coach@bigpond.com or you can download copies from www.presentperfect.com.au

Example #1 Worksheet A2 – Exploring my energy drains

	Self care isn't selfish
P	Worksheet A2: Exploring my energy drains (What is easy to let go of and what would be the benefits?)

Write a brief description of a situation you've identified as an energy drain and then ask yourself the questions below.

Brief description of energy drain

I'm spending way too much time listening to my work colleague's personal problems. This makes me feel depleted and frustrated because they don't take my advice and don't seem to want to resolve anything, just complain.

How hard does it feel to let go of this?

This feels fairly difficult but not impossible. People just seem to gravitate towards me and pour out their problems. I'm a good listener and I'd feel unkind, and perhaps ashamed, if I stopped trying to help them.

How would I feel better if I let it go?

I'd feel HEAPS better - I wouldn't feel depleted or frustrated. I'd be more able to complete my tasks during work hours and wouldn't need to take work home. This could give me an extra two to four hours each working week.

Example #2 Worksheet A2 – Exploring my energy drains

Self care isn't selfish

P

Worksheet A2: What is easy to let go of and what would be the benefits?

Write a brief description of a situation you've identified as an energy drain and then ask yourself the questions below.

Brief description of energy drain

When I do get some time for myself, I feel too unmotivated to do anything much and end up wasting time on the internet or falling asleep in front of the TV. I feel guilty and annoyed with myself.

How hard does it feel to let go of this?

I'm embarrassed to admit that this feels hard. It should be easy. If I were to try to change and fail, I'd feel even worse about myself.

How would I feel better if I let it go?

This would be a huge win – I would feel better about myself and could enjoy doing something productive, inspiring, enjoyable and restful.

Example #3 Worksheet A2 – Exploring my energy drains

P Self care isn't selfish

Worksheet A2: What is easy to let go of and what would be the benefits?

Write a brief description of a situation you've identified as an energy drain and then ask yourself the questions below.

Brief description of energy drain

I often find myself volunteering to help out and end up doing more than my fair share of the work. I'm usually the one who ends up taking all the girls to their soccer games every week. This brings up resentment and exhaustion.

How hard does it feel to let go of this?

This feels fairly easy. I've had enough of feeling 'used'! Many of the activities I do, e.g. arranging activities for the work social club, are not really that important to me. Jane won't mind if I don't go to every soccer game.

How would I feel better if I let it go?

This would free up a lot of time and energy and stop me from feeling 'used'.

Acknowledge yourself, take break. When you're ready, we'll move on to identify what changes you're ready to commit to.

Reader activity #3:
What am I ready to commit to?

As you move on to the next activity (worksheet A3), be prepared to ask yourself questions and explore what's happening. Choose just one or two energy drains that feel easy to address and one or two which will give you substantial benefits. We are looking for doable steps and positive benefits, not just a journal or completed workbook. For these, ask yourself:

What is this telling me? What are the possible actions available to me? What am I ready to commit to? What skills and support do I need? What belief systems do I need to change or bring on board?

To help you to complete the worksheet, we'll review how to work with the three important signposts, The Shire of Should, Passive Aggressive Trap and Resentment Road.

'Shoulds' are those things which, for some reason, you feel you should be doing, but on deeper examination you discover that they're not really important to you. Perhaps you feel you should attend every work function or you should produce a gourmet meal every time someone comes to dinner. Overwhelm is often a sign of unclear values, unsure what is actually important to you. Perhaps there are too many shoulds taking up your time. The test is to see whether you can genuinely replace the words 'I should' with 'I truly want to'.

'I've seen women insist on cleaning everything in the house before they could sit down to write... and you know it's a funny thing about housecleaning... it never comes to an end. Perfect way to stop a woman. A woman must be careful to not allow over-responsibility (or over-respectability) to steal her necessary creative rests, riffs, and raptures. She simply must put her foot down and say no to half of what she believes she 'should' be doing. Art is not meant to be created in stolen moments only.'

Clarissa Pinkola Estés, author

The shoulds probably began in your childhood, or maybe they're a product of the society you live in. Perhaps, with a change of attitude, some support and a bit of practice, you could eliminate these activities completely.

'Be Yourself. Everyone else is taken.'

Oscar Wilde, Author

Let's look at the areas where you feel as though your efforts are being unappreciated - the areas around Passive Aggressive Trap. Why are they unappreciated? If we are not getting acknowledgement for what we are doing for others, it probably means that they don't value what we're giving them. We can stop giving it, they will be just as happy, they really don't care whether it's done or not.

For example, your children probably don't see any value in a clean floor. We tend to give what we want for ourselves. It's so much easier to just ask for what we want. Consider whether your children are old enough to take on some cleaning tasks themselves. It's likely that they won't do it as well as you would, but is this, perhaps, a life skill they need to learn?

> 'Exactly what are you wanting to teach your children? How to love and care for themselves, or how to neglect and abandon themselves? Self-sacrifice is NOT setting a good example.'
>
> Miya Yamanouchi, counsellor

There are many other options you might consider: Do you want to accept a messy floor in exchange for some more time? Do you want to employ a cleaner, resulting in a clean floor and more time in exchange for cash?

Another option might be to consider whether you would enjoy both having a clean and tidy environment and doing the cleaning and tidying. Strange as it might seem, if you gave up any expectation of thanks or appreciation, you might find that you actually enjoy cleaning and tidying as a form of mental relaxation.

> 'If you don't like something, change it. If you can't change it, change your attitude. Don't complain.'
>
> Maya Angelou, author

Look at the areas where resentment is creeping in. We need to remember that feeling a little resentful (or even a lot!) does not make us a bad person. This feeling is telling us something very useful. It's telling us that someone else is experiencing something we want for ourselves, and it feels like it is at our expense. Maybe you feel resentful that others are getting what you would dearly love and possibly really need for yourself. Twenty minutes sitting on the couch might be exactly what you need right now.

Depression and lack of motivation might indicate you are bored. Perhaps you are stuck in old habits which are no longer serving you.

'If you do not change direction,
you may end up where you are heading.'
Lao Tzu, philosopher and poet

Example #1 Worksheet A3 –
What am I ready to commit to?

P Self care isn't selfish

Worksheet A3: What am I ready to commit to?

Write a brief description of a situation you've identified as an energy drain and then answer the questions below.

Brief description of the energy drain

I'm spending way too much time listening to my work colleague's personal problems. This makes me feel depleted and frustrated because she doesn't take my advice and doesn't seem to want to resolve anything, just complain.

How hard does it feel to let go of this?

This feels fairly hard but not impossible. People seem to gravitate towards me and pour out their problems. I'm a good listener and I would feel unkind, and perhaps ashamed, if I stopped trying to help them.

How would I feel better if I let it go?

I'd feel much better - I wouldn't feel depleted or frustrated, I'd be more able to complete my work tasks well during work hours and wouldn't need to take work home. This would probably give me an extra 2 to 4 hours each working week.

What is this telling me?

I feel frustrated and depleted because they don't take my advice and don't seem to want to resolve anything, just complain. Being a good listener is a skill of which I'm justly proud. Is shame suggesting that some of my own self-worth is tied up in this perhaps? Have I taken on a 'should' here - that I should be available to help everyone?

Some people just need to be heard. If I have the time to listen I can do this to help my colleague. Spending time trying to fix her problems is a waste of my time and energy and it is not helping her.

What are the possible actions available to me?

- Shut my office door more often.
- Run when I see her coming!
- I could listen without saying anything, I could nod and smile to show I am listening and not make suggestions or give advice.

What am I ready to commit to?

I'm ready to commit to not giving any advice and learning to listen without offering sympathetic comments which prolong the conversation.

What support do I need?

I think I just need practice or maybe a reminder on my computer - Don't give advice when none is wanted.

I wonder how everyone else in the office responds to her? Perhaps I can learn something from them?

What belief systems do I need to change or bring on board?

I am worthy. I do not need to fix everyone's problems in order to be worthy of respect.

'Ours is not the task of fixing the entire world at once, but of stretching out to mend the part of the world that is within our reach.'

Clarissa Pinkola Estés, author

Example #2 Worksheet A3 – What am I ready to commit to?

P Self care isn't selfish

Worksheet A3: What am I ready to commit to?

Write a brief description of a situation you've identified as an energy drain and then answer the questions below.

Brief description of the energy drain

When I do get some time for myself I feel too **unmotivated** to do anything much and end up wasting time on the internet or falling asleep in front of the telly. I feel **guilty and annoyed with myself.**

How hard does it feel to let go of this?

I feel embarrassed to admit that this feels hard. It should be easy. If I try to change and fail, I'll feel even worse about myself.

How would I feel better if I let it go?

This would be a huge win - I would feel better about myself and could have two or more hours per night to do something productive, inspiring, enjoyable and restful.

What is this telling me?

Why do I waste time and then beat myself up? There is shame around this and I feel that I am not good enough and lack will power.

Am I so tired that I am approaching Depression Swamp? Do I need rest?

Am I bored? I think I've forgotten what it is I actually enjoy doing and maybe I feel I don't deserve to enjoy myself.

What are the possible actions available to me?

- If I'm tired I could go to bed early, I could put on some music and light some candles and have a bath.

- If I'm bored I could try something new: an exercise class, learn something new or read something inspiring.

What am I ready to commit to?

- Recognising the shame trigger - and giving myself permission to be kind to myself.

- Commit to following through on the exercises in this book.

- Make a list of the things I enjoy doing and add them into my do list.

What support do I need?

This would be easier if I make a commitment to someone else, perhaps if I pay for a term of art classes or find an exercise buddy. I might need someone independent who will support me and hold me accountable.

What belief systems do I need to change or bring on board?

I need to dump some shame. I deserve to treat myself with more respect and care.

Example #3 Worksheet A3 –
What am I ready to commit to?

P Self care isn't selfish

Worksheet A3: What am I ready to commit to?

Write a brief description of a situation you've identified as an energy drain and then answer the questions below.

Brief description of the energy drain

I often find myself volunteering to help out and end up doing more than my fair share of the work. I'm usually the one who ends up taking all the girls to their soccer games every week. This brings up **resentment** and **exhaustion**.

How hard does it feel to let go of this?

This feels fairly easy. I've had enough of feeling used. Many of the activities that I do, e.g. arranging activities for the work social club, are not really that important to me. Jane won't mind if I don't go to every soccer game.

How would I feel better if I let it go?

This would free up a lot of time and energy and stop me from feeling used.

What is this telling me?

I am on Resentment Road. I need to stop volunteering to do things which make me feel used. I can still volunteer and help out on some things - but not everything!

What are the possible actions available to me?

I could stop taking the girls to the games and ask the other parents to do it.

I could take the girls to two or three games out of every four.

I could stop myself from volunteering for the work social club.

What am I ready to commit to?

Ask the other parents to take the girls to every fourth game.

Practice not volunteering for the social club.

What support do I need?

I need Jane's support and understanding.

What belief systems do I need to change or bring on board?

Self care isn't selfish, I can ask for what I want.

Lessons from Chapter Four

If something drains me, then it drains me. There is no need to feel embarrassed, nor any need to justify.

I will start by using the 80/20 rule to get the biggest benefits for the least amount of effort.

There are often many possible courses of action I could take to reduce my energy drains. I could change my actions or my beliefs.

I will decide which actions I am ready to commit to.

I will make sure I identify the support I need.

Chapter Five

What nourishes you?
Filling up your Self Care Wells.

So, now that you have identified some things you are going to stop doing, or going to do less of, I hope you feel ready to identify what you would like to do for yourself in the time that you have retrieved.

> 'When you recover or discover
> something that nourishes your soul
> and brings joy, care enough about yourself
> to make room for it in your life.'
>
> Jean Shinoda Bolen, author

What would you like to have available in your Self Care Wells? What nourishes you?

It makes sense to have a variety of options to draw from your well. Sometimes you might have an hour or even a whole day; time for a good long drink from your well. More often you'll have 15 minutes or 30 seconds, just enough time for a quick sip. Spending a whole day pampering at a spa or an afternoon playing golf might be a great way to nurture yourself. However, my sense is that self care is found mostly in the small moments, those times when you take 30 seconds for two deep breaths or five minutes to write in a gratitude diary before bed.

'To experience peace does not mean that your life is always blissful. It means that you are capable of tapping into a blissful state of mind amidst the normal chaos of a hectic life.'

Jill Bolte Taylor, neuroanatomist, author, speaker

Sometimes you might want to spend time alone, sometimes the right company might be more nourishing, sometimes you might want to be physically active, sometimes emotionally restful. What we are looking for is a wide range of nourishment for your mind, body and spirit.

Signposts that might suggest what you need

The signpost of resentment can sometimes give you a clue as to what you need to put into your Self Care Wells. What are you giving to others that isn't being appreciated? Is this something that you would love to do for yourself?

The signpost of physical exhaustion suggests you need to stock your wells with physical rest and rejuvenation - maybe this means a yin yoga class or a massage each week, maybe a commitment to an earlier bed time, or accepting that the house is a mess and having a nap when the baby is asleep.

The signpost of sadness, despair or depression might suggest that you need some spiritual nourishment and physical activity - maybe listening to an inspirational podcast, watching a sunset, playing with the dog, surfing, swimming. Maybe your creative self needs to be allowed some time to paint, write or perhaps even dance.

The signpost of overwhelm might suggest you need some mental rest; perhaps some physical 'mindless' activity, maybe a run, or a walk in nature, or even tidying up a kitchen drawer. It's amazing how cleaning or clearing out physical stuff can help to clear the mental stuff.

The signpost of boredom might suggest that you would benefit from adding more complexity and variety into your life. Perhaps learning a language or studying something you have always been interested in but never allowed yourself the time to explore.

Remember, these are just my suggestions and I encourage you to learn to listen to your mind, body and spirit, to learn to read your signposts and experiment with your responses.

'If you would shut your door against the children for an hour a day and say; "Mother is working on her five-act tragedy in blank verse!" you would be surprised how they would respect you. They would probably all become playwrights.'

Brenda Ueland, writer, author, teacher

As you think about what you might like, I encourage you ignore those things you think you should be choosing, and identify what it is you really want for yourself. Let's consider a typical example of getting fitter. Our first thought might be to join the gym or go for a run every morning. This may truly be an act of self care and you know that you would feel more vibrant if you improved your fitness, but what do we do if these options feel like a should, rather than a pleasure? For many of us, the thought of a brightly lit gym with huge mirrors, loud music, surrounded by slim young people in the latest work out gear feels more like a source of stress rather than self care. So, if this resonates with you, I suggest that you're going to have a much better chance of improving your fitness if you take the time to consider how you might be able to make this fun, or at least not feel like a punishment. Think about how you could fit this into other self care activities. If you enjoy being part of a team or would like more company, then perhaps joining a local hockey team might be fun. If you would love some time alone in nature, perhaps some long walks through the countryside would be a good start towards your fitness goal.

'Dancing in the dark at No Lights No Lycra has been the only kind of exercise in the past 10 years I've absolutely and unequivocally loved. I come home buzzing - physically and emotionally rejuvenated.'

Lisa, Melbourne

Reader Activity #3: Filling your Self Care Wells

Using worksheet B from Resources, begin to put together some ideas for your Self Care Wells. Identify what constitutes self care for you. What brings you pleasure? What rejuvenates you? Remember, these are activities to restore your mind, body and spirit; for when your mind feels overwhelmed; for when your body is tired; for when you feel sad or empty.

If you can't think of anything, don't panic and don't give up on yourself. I've worked with clients who looked at me blankly when I asked what gives them pleasure and said: "I don't know any more, I guess I used to have fun, once". If you really can't think of anything, that's okay. As you start to let go of some of the things that drain you, it will become easier to identify what you might need or enjoy.

> 'For a toddler's mum, a shower is the equivalent of a visit to a day spa.'
>
> Lou, life coaching client

Here's an example. (Remember, this is just an example and your list may look very different.)

Example #1 Worksheet B – Self Care Wells

P Self care isn't selfish
Worksheet B: Self Care Wells

**Ask yourself: What do I enjoy doing? What brings me pleasure?
What brings me energy? What makes me smile? What makes me feel better?**

Quick Sips

Taking 2 deep breaths

Breathe for 30 seconds

Sitting in the garden or a park for 10 minutes

Expressing gratitude

Filling the house with flowers

Good Long Drinks

Sitting in a café and writing

Sketching

A weekend in the country

Yoga

Going for a run

Going to bed earlier and reading a good book

Having friends round for a pot luck dinner

Learning to paint with watercolours

Watching a funny movie

Going on a media fast: no Facebook, no newspapers, no watching or listening to the news

Taking a lunch break - getting away from the desk and eating something nutritious

Having a foot massage

Going for a long walk along the beach

Now that you have your list, perhaps you can find a way to be creative and design a self care project that satisfies a number of your desires? For example, if you'd enjoy some intellectual stimulation, love gardening, would like some more physical activity, care about the environment and would enjoy the company of like-minded people, then you could:

Take a permaculture design course, join a local community garden or environmental group, contribute photographs and articles to the group's blog, and get some exercise weeding and digging. Who knows where this might lead!

Lessons from Chapter Five

It's important to identify activities which I can use to restore my energy and wellbeing - contents for my Self Care Wells.

It's okay if I don't know what these are yet, I will stay alert to noticing, remembering and identifying what it is that brings me pleasure and restores me.

Self care is found mostly in the small everyday moments. I shall include activities to bring me: rest, enthusiasm, joy, inspiration, creative outlets, nourishment, exercise - physical, mental, spiritual and emotional.

With some creative thinking I can design self care activities which avoid any 'shoulds'.

Chapter Six
Living in The Heartlands

So now that you have:

- A feel for the map and the warning signs that indicate you are moving into self-neglect.
- Made commitments to reduce change or eliminate some activities.
- Identified new mindsets, the support you need and nourishment for your self care wells.

It's time to put it all into action.

Your action plan

For your journey away from the Land of Self Neglect and around The Heartlands, you'll need actions and habits to support you as you:

- Let go of some activities and unhelpful beliefs.
- Add in new self care activities.
- Add in helpful beliefs and support systems.
- Become aware of signposts which tell you when to pause, when to change direction and when to visit a Self Care Well.

Remember, we are not going for a goal. We're changing our way of being in the world. This means that, as well as doing specific one-off tasks or activities you will also be developing new habits.

A word on habits

According to the Society for Personality and Social Psychology, up to 40% of our behaviour is habitual.

> 'Much of our daily lives are taken up by habits that we've formed over our lifetime. An important characteristic of a habit is that it's automatic – we don't always recognize habits in our own behavior. Studies show that about 40 percent of people's daily activities are performed each day in almost the same situations.'
>
> Society for Personality and Social Psychology

So, if up to 40% of what we do is habit, it makes sense to develop new habits to support our commitment to balancing self care with care for others.

We all come across people who have a profound influence on our life. For me, one such teacher is Sonia Choquette. She introduced me to the concept of the subconscious as a 'co-operative four year old who wants to please'. Say to a four year old, "This house is a *mess*, you *never* put your things away. I've got friends coming round this evening and there is *nowhere* for them to sit. I do *everything* around here, and *nobody* helps"' Do you think they are going to help you tidy up? Say to a co-operative four year old, "Please take your toys off the chair and put them in your toy box", and they will do it. So it is with the subconscious; you need to make your requests to yourself simple, clear, kind and achievable.

Choose one of your intentions, something you want to change in your ways of being. Let's use our example of practicing saying no to unreasonable requests for your time. Craft a baby step, or series of baby steps, which will make saying no, in a kind and easy way, a natural part of who you are. The first step might be to pause when someone requests your time, breathe in and out and say, "Let me check my diary and get back to you". The key is to make this habit simple, achievable, not too much effort, and really clear. In this instance, we have a ready-made "trigger" to alert us, i.e. someone is asking for our time. For other habits we want to develop, there may not be any external trigger. In these instances, it might help you if you tie in each one of your intended new habits with something that is already a habit for you. If you often put the kettle on, this could be your reminder to check in with how you're feeling; if you check that all the lights are off before you go to bed, this could be your cue to bring to mind five things that made you smile today.

Reader activity #4:
Write down a list of your new habits

Imagine that you are going to take a week off from your life, and that I'm going to take your place and be you for this week. Write all your new habits down in a way that I would be able to step up and know exactly what to do to be you.

Remember, an activity becomes a habit when our subconscious just gets on with it. If, after three or four weeks, these baby steps have not become automatic and don't look as though they are going to be, then choose some new ones to support your intention. Once you've found one that works for you, and you are doing it as automatically as brushing your teeth, then you can take it off your list. Celebrate, and then consider whether you would like to add another supportive habit to move you further along your journey. It's simple, and it works!

If you enjoy ticking things off your to do list, make sure these habits are on your list. Take pleasure from ticking them off.

'All our life ...
is but a mass of habits.'
William James, 19th century psychologist

A word on actions (deadlines and accountability)

We each have our own way of planning our actions and activities, and if you have a way that works well for you there may be no need to change your method. However, with your existing actions, e.g. attend project meeting, 2pm Tuesday 15th or buy milk on way home tonight, there are often external deadlines and others depending on you achieving them. For some of your new self care actions, there is less chance that there will be any external pressure or deadline to meet. For this reason I encourage you to schedule, not just write a to-do list. Give yourself some deadlines and accountability. Actions such as attend yoga class Tuesday, and research art classes need to be in your diary - in ink! If you're a visual person you might like to try colour coding. Choose a colour to mark out time to look after yourself. A glance in your diary should make it clear whether you're balancing your time and energy appropriately. Make it a priority to keep your commitments to yourself.

A word on support systems

Remember to work with your support team. Having someone to champion you, encourage you, celebrate with you and hold you accountable can be extremely helpful. In Chapter 3 we discussed some of the road hazards you are likely to encounter on your way back to The Heartlands, places where you may stumble and feel tempted to give up or take rash actions which you may regret later. Your journey will be smoother if you have a good support team in place to help you along. You might like to think of your Self Care Wells being surrounded by a village green, and your support team members as villagers whom you can meet there for encouragement and help.

Building your support team might be simply a case of having conversations with your spouse, family, friends and workmates and letting them know that you are taking this journey. You may like to find a self-care buddy, perhaps a friend who is ready to take their own journey back to The Heartlands and will join you on your daily walk or weekly art class. What I want for you is that you hold yourself in enough esteem that you can always keep your commitments to yourself (and yet I acknowledge that it is easier to keep commitments to others than it is to keep commitments to our self). For some of your aims, you might also choose to put more formal support in place, perhaps a nutritionist, a personal trainer or a life coach.

'A life coach is someone who believes
in your dream and sings it to you
when you have forgotten the words.'
Susie Ascott

A word on belief systems

Consider how you are going to integrate your new belief systems. Do affirmations work for you? One client finds it very effective to write out her affirmations and put them up on the walls around her house. Another client finds this irritating and unhelpful.

Take a bit of time to decide what might work best for you as you begin to let go of unhelpful belief systems and adopt supportive ones. Speaking affirmations out loud, while looking at yourself in a mirror, might work for you. If, however, you have a visceral negative reaction, or you find yourself mentally disagreeing, I believe affirmations can do more harm than good. It might feel as if you are lying to yourself and subconsciously you are learning to distrust yourself. Aspirations might work better for you. For example, instead of saying, "I deserve to be kind to myself" you might start by saying, "I'd like to believe that I deserve to be kind to myself". Once you feel totally comfortable with this then you can change it to, "I'm starting to believe that I deserve to be kind to myself", then "I deserve to be kind to myself", then "I aspire to be kind to myself" until you can happily say "I am happy that I am kind to myself".

Creating your plan

So, are you ready to create your plan? Here's an example.

Self care isn't selfish

Worksheet C: My action plan

Habit	When
Check in with what I am feeling and practice interpreting the signs.	Whenever I can. Until this becomes a habit I will add this to any existing habit or regular activity, e.g. when I walk from one room to another, when I put the kettle on for a cup of tea, when I finish a phone call, when I am brushing my teeth. Whenever I notice I am feeling less than content.
Practice recognising the 'shame' triggers and responding with self-compassion.	Whenever I feel less than adequate or guilty.
Take 2 deep breaths.	Before answering the phone Before speaking
Sit in the garden or the park, somewhere in nature, for 10 mins every day.	Lunch time
Listen to my complaining work colleague without adding to the conversation and without offering advice.	Whenever she complains

Ask every member of the family, including myself, to list two or three good things that happened in their day, things they are grateful for or happy about.	Before dinner (a secular form of saying grace)
Buy or pick some flowers for the house.	Wednesday evening when I buy the groceries.
Say "I'll check my diary and get back to you".	Whenever anyone asks for my time.
Go to bed early and read a good book.	When I notice myself 'wasting' time on Facebook or watching rubbish on TV.
Schedule ALL activities in my diary. Use green ink for my self care activities (green feels like a nourishing colour to mark out me-time).	Add things in as I commit to them and review diary every Sunday evening after my weekly phone call to Mum.

Actions

Talk with other soccer mums and work out a roster. Talk with Jane and explain that I won't be going to every game.	Next Saturday
Watch how others deal with complaining colleague.	Ongoing
Go to café and write journal.	Every fourth Saturday morning.
Take pencils and sketch pad with me to soccer games. Give myself permission to sketch badly. It's the process, not the product that matters.	Every soccer game

Research watercolour classes.	By 10th Aug
Write out new belief systems and put them next to bathroom mirror.	This Friday
Find a yoga class on Thursday evenings - ask Mary if she would like to go with me.	By 15th August
Talk with my sister and see if she would be prepared to be my self care buddy.	When I see her next Sunday.

Lessons from Chapter Six

We are creatures of habit. I shall use this as a strength as I create new habits to support myself.

I can develop supportive belief systems.

Small consistent steps will get me there.

I will schedule my new habits and actions.

My self care activities are high priority.

I will hold myself accountable and use my support team.

Chapter 7
Summing up

Whilst this little book is about self care, we could equally say that it is about self kindfulness or **mindfully choosing** to be kind to ourselves whenever we can. I hope that my words have reminded you that kindfulness begins through consciously developing self care habits and that these are far from selfish.

I hope you've had some breakthroughs and realisations that have sparked positive change. Perhaps you've had a weekend without housework or got back to activities that bring you joy.

'I've been making further changes and had a cleaner come in last week for the first time in three years. I can't tell you how light I felt after that, knowing that I wouldn't have to spend the weekend with the hoover out, nagging my kids to dust their desks.'

Lisa, Melbourne

Making changes in your belief systems and thinking patterns will lead you back towards The Heartlands. Huge benefits can come from learning to be aware of the signs of self neglect and catching and directing your thinking away from the Well-Worn Pathways.

> 'Your advice on how to manage my thoughts and feelings has totally changed my approach to our marriage and it is better than it has ever been.'
>
> N.H, coaching client, Western Australia

Stocking our Self Care Wells and visiting them regularly will ensure we have the energy to continue our journey as we build new habits and pathways back to The Heartlands.

> 'With your help I have now brought writing, gratitude list and prayer to my everyday life. For the past weeks I have come back to reading books and I practice yoga every second day. I love it and all this makes me feel so good. For the first time in 10 years I fall asleep within minutes after going to bed.'
>
> Johanna, coaching client, Finland

By learning and applying the strategies in this book you will become, more and more, the kind and caring person you truly are. From a grounding of self care you will have the vitality, enthusiasm and time to enjoy your life - with plenty of vitality, enthusiasm and time left over to spread this joy and be there for others. This is what I want for us all.

'I'm happier and I'm finding my way. I'm making big changes within myself. It's a feeling of everything falling in to place. It's wonderful.'

J.T, coaching client, Western Australia

This book is designed as a roadmap, a guidebook, something you can read through, but more importantly, refer to as you travel through your life. I encourage you to call upon this book and the map any time you feel or see the signs of self neglect. Take the time to assess what's going on for you, before consciously choosing your next step.

Remember to take one step at a time, have patience with yourself and with the process. The more you practice, the easier and more natural it will become.

May you enjoy your journey back to, and around, The Heartlands. I would love you to keep in touch and let me know how you are going and I look forward to celebrating with you.

My new belief systems

Self care is not selfish - it is taking responsibility for my own happiness. Self care is an important part of my life.

Self care gives me the energy and nourishment I need to achieve great things. It's the basis for my wellbeing. Self neglect makes me vulnerable to selfish behaviour. I can use my existing skills to be kind to myself. I can choose to change outdated or unhelpful belief systems. It's okay to stumble occasionally, to forgive myself, and be my own best friend. It's important, and kind, to ask for what I want and accept the help of my support team.

My new habits

Eliminate, reduce, change the activities that drain me. Add in activities that nourish me. Take the time to listen to the messages from my mind, body and spirit.

Question myself to discover what I can change in my behaviour, thoughts and belief systems. Practice patience and take one step at a time. Review progress weekly.

My personal plan

1. Write down the activities that drain me (Worksheet A1 - Identifying my energy drains).

2. Identify the benefits and effort involved in reducing or eliminating each energy drain (Worksheet A2 - Exploring my energy drains).

3. Decide what changes I'm ready to commit to, the belief systems I need to take on board and the support I need to put in place to achieve results (Worksheet A3 - What am I ready to commit to?).

4. Write down content for my Self Care Wells (Worksheet B – Self Care Wells).

5. Identify my new habits, clearly defined as small, consistent steps (Worksheet C - My action plan).

6. Write down my required actions (Worksheet C - My action plan).

7. Transfer habits and actions to my to-do list and/or schedule in my diary - in ink.

8. Review weekly, celebrate progress and add new habits and actions as I travel towards and within The Heartlands.

Selected resources
References, recommended reading & listening

Here you will find references used in this book, suggestions for further reading and resources you might enjoy if you are keen to do more research. The worksheets used in this book can also be found in this section.

I encourage you to contact me if you have any feedback, questions or suggestions. You can do so directly via email susie_coach@bigpond.com or via my website www.presentperfect.com.au

Chapter One

- Thich Nhat Hanh,
  http://plumvillage.org/about/thich-nhat-hanh

Chapter Two

- Clarissa Pinkola Estes, 1992, *Women Who Run With the Wolves: Myths and Stories of the Wild Woman Archetype*, Rider, London

- Etty Hillesum, Worked in "Social Welfare for People in Transit" during the holocaust, died at Auschwitz c. 30 November 1943 https://en.wikipedia.org/wiki/Etty_Hillesum

- George Bernard Shaw, http://www.biography.com/people/george-bernard-shaw-9480925

- Susan Solomon, https://www.linkedin.com/pub/susan-solomon/18/7ab/605 http://www.bustle.com/articles/18535-how-to-stop-being-passive-aggressive-in-5-relatively-simple-steps

- Amanda Palmer, 2014, *The Art of Asking; or, How I Learned to Stop Worrying and Let People Help,* Grand Central Publishing, New York City

- Ralph Waldo Emerson, http://transcendentalism-legacy.tamu.edu/authors/emerson/

- Deborah Day, clinician in the mental health field, http://www.deborahdayma.com

Chapter Three

- Anne Wilson Schaef, http://www.livinginprocess.com/index.php

- Max Ehrmann, http://www.aumara.com/inspirations/authors/mehrmann.html

- Maya Angelou, http://mayaangelou.com/

- A.C. Benson, http://www.thefamouspeople.com/profiles/arthur-christopher-benson-599.php

Chapter Four

- Clarissa Pinkola Estes, 1992, *Women Who Run With the Wolves: Myths and Stories of the Wild Woman Archetype*, Rider, London

- Oscar Wilde, http://www.biography.com/people/oscar-wilde-9531078

- Miya Yamanouchi, 2015, *Embrace Your Sexual Self: A Practical Guide for Women*, Booktango e-book

- Maya Angelou, http://mayaangelou.com/

- Lao Tzu, http://thephilosophersmail.com/perspective/the-great-eastern-philosophers-lao-tzu/

- Pareto Principle (80/20 rule) http://betterexplained.com/articles/understanding-the-pareto-principle-the-8020-rule/

Chapter Five

- Jean Shinoda Bolen, http://www.jeanbolen.com/

- Jill Bolte Taylor, http://drjilltaylor.com/

- Brenda Ueland, https://en.wikipedia.org/wiki/Brenda_Ueland

Chapter Six

- Society for Personality and Social Psychology, http://www.spsp.org/news-center/press-releases/how-we-form-habits-and-change-existing-ones

- Sonia Choquette, http://www.soniachoquette.com/

- William James, http://psychology.about.com/od/profilesofmajorthinkers/p/jamesbio.htm

Suggested further learning

Empathy: Karla McLaren

- *Emotional Flow, Becoming Fluent in the Language of Emotions,* 2012, Online course, http://karlamclaren.com/our-online-course-is-here-emotional-flow/

- *The Language of Emotions, What Your Feelings Are Trying to Tell You,* 2010, Book and audio learning program, http://karlamclaren.com/bookshop/books-and-audio/

- *The Art of Empathy, A Complete Guide to Life's Most Essential Skill, 2013,* Book and audio learning program, http://www.soundstrue.com/store/the-art-of-empathy-3367.html

Shame: Brene Brown

- *The Power of Vulnerability, Teachings on Authenticity, Connection, and Courage,* 2013, CD/Audio, Sounds True Inc, Louisville Co, USA http://www.soundstrue.com/store/the-power-of-vulnerability-2917.html

- *Men, Women and Worthiness, The Experience of Shame and the Power of Being Enough,* 2012, CD/Audio, Sounds True Inc, Louisville Co, USA http://www.soundstrue.com/store/men-women-and-worthiness-2911.html

Self Compassion: Pema Chodron

- *Getting Unstuck,* 2005, CD/Audio, Sounds True Inc, Louisville Co, USA http://www.soundstrue.com/store/getting-unstuck-3900.html

- *The Freedom to Love, An Online Training Course to Liberate Your Genuine Heart,* 2012, Self guided video course, Sounds True Inc, Louisville Co, USA http://www.soundstrue.com/store/the-freedom-to-love-2397.html

- *Self Compassion,* 1999, CD/Audio, Pema Chodron Foundation http://pemachodronfoundation.org/product/self-compassion/

Meditation:

- Pema Chodron is an American Buddhist nun. She has written several books: *The Wisdom of No Escape*, *Start Where You Are*, *When Things Fall Apart*, *The Places that Scare You*, *No Time to Lose*, *Practicing Peace in Times of War*, and *Smile at Fear*. She runs retreats and is a sought after speaker. Her compassionate, humorous and pragmatic approach makes her teachings very accessible. http://pemachodronfoundation.org/about/pema-chodron/

- Jon Kabat-Zinn is Professor of Medicine Emeritus and creator of the Stress Reduction Clinic and the Center for Mindfulness in Medicine, Health Care, and Society at the University of Massachusetts Medical School. His approach to Mindfulness Meditation is secular, making his teachings widely accessible. http://www.mindful.org/jon-kabat-zinn-video-series-on-mindful-org/

Rick Hanson, Ph.D., is a psychologist, Senior Fellow of the Greater Good Science Center at UC Berkeley, and best-selling author. He is the founder of the Wellspring Institute for Neuroscience and Contemplative Wisdom, he has taught in meditation centres worldwide. His approach to mindfulness meditation is secular, making his teachings highly accessible to all. http/:ww.rickhanson.net/

Further free resources from the author

Send an email to susie_coach@bigpond.com and claim:

a) Your printable copy of the Self Care Map, in colour.

b) Your downloadable copies of the worksheets used in this book.

c) Your complimentary 1 hour coaching session, via phone or skype.

Ongoing support

Visit **www.presentperfect.com.au** or email me at susie_coach@bigpond.com for information on ongoing life coaching and an online self care course based on the learning and practices in this book.

Worksheet A1 –
Identifying my energy drains

P Self care isn't selfish

Worksheet A1: Identifying my energy drains
(What drains me?)

Ask yourself the questions below and then write a brief description of each activity or situation and its consequence on your energy levels.

Where am I over-extending my time and energy?

What signs of self-neglect are showing up?

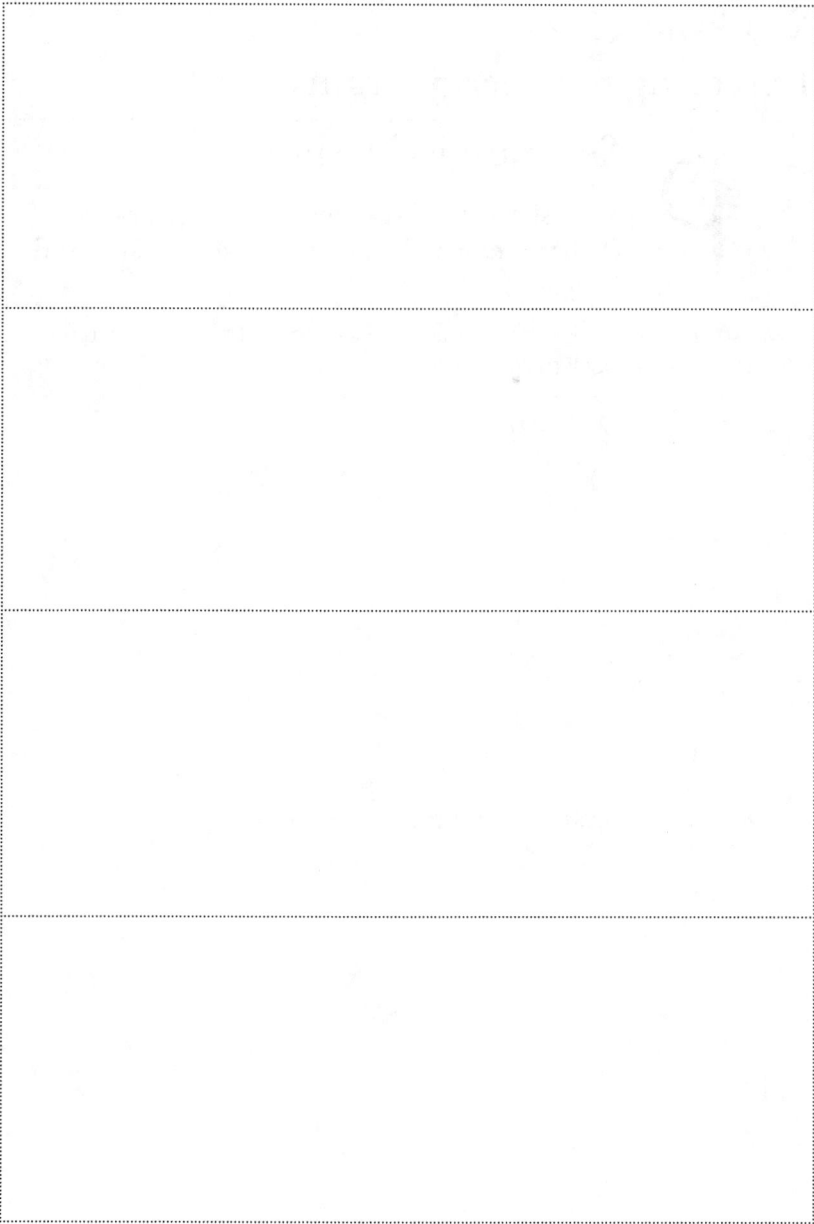

Worksheet A2 –
Exploring my energy drains

Self care isn't selfish

Worksheet A2: Exploring my energy drains
(What is easy to let go of and what would be the benefits?)

Write a brief description of a situation you've identified as an energy drain and then ask yourself the questions below.

Brief description of energy drain

How hard does it feel to let go of this?

How would I feel better if I let it go?

Worksheet A2 –
Exploring my energy drains

Self care isn't selfish

Worksheet A2: Exploring my energy drains
(What is easy to let go of and what would be the benefits?)

Write a brief description of a situation you've identified as an energy drain and then ask yourself the questions below.

Brief description of energy drain

How hard does it feel to let go of this?

How would I feel better if I let it go?

Worksheet A2 –
Exploring my energy drains

Self care isn't selfish

Worksheet A2: Exploring my energy drains
(What is easy to let go of and what would be the
benefits?)

Write a brief description of a situation you've identified as an energy drain
and then ask yourself the questions below.

Brief description of energy drain

How hard does it feel to let go of this?

How would I feel better if I let it go?

Worksheet A2 – Exploring my energy drains

Self care isn't selfish

Worksheet A2: Exploring my energy drains
(What is easy to let go of and what would be the benefits?)

Write a brief description of a situation you've identified as an energy drain and then ask yourself the questions below.

Brief description of energy drain

How hard does it feel to let go of this?

How would I feel better if I let it go?

For more worksheets in which to explore your energy drains,
email me at susie_coach@bigpond.com

Worksheet A3 –
What am I ready to commit to?

Self care isn't selfish

Worksheet A3: What am I ready to commit to?

Write a brief description of a situation you've identified as an energy drain and then ask yourself the questions below.

Brief description of energy drain

How hard does it feel to let go of this?

How would I feel better if I let it go?

What is this telling me?

What are the possible actions available to me?

What am I ready to commit to?

What support do I need?

What belief systems do I need to change or bring on board?

Worksheet A3 –
What am I ready to commit to?

P | Self care isn't selfish

Worksheet A3: What am I ready to commit to?

Write a brief description of a situation you've identified as an energy drain and then ask yourself the questions below.

Brief description of energy drain

How hard does it feel to let go of this?

How would I feel better if I let it go?

What is this telling me?

What are the possible actions available to me?

What am I ready to commit to?

What support do I need?

What belief systems do I need to change or bring on board?

For more worksheets in which to explore what you are ready to commit to, email me at susie_coach@bigpond.com

Worksheet B – Self Care Wells

P Self care isn't selfish
Worksheet B: Self Care Wells

Ask yourself: What do I enjoy doing? What brings me pleasure?
What brings me energy? What makes me smile? What makes me feel better?

Quick Sips

Good Long Drinks

Worksheet C – My action plan

Self care isn't selfish

Worksheet C: My action plan

Habit	When
Check in with what I am feeling and practice interpreting the signs.	Whenever I can. Until this becomes a habit I will add this to any existing habit or regular activity, e.g. when I walk from one room to another, when I put the kettle on for a cup of tea, when I finish a phone call, when I am brushing my teeth.

Actions	By When

Acknowledgements

I wish to thank Lisa, for her advice and encouragement, turning my thoughts into sentences, and Sharon for her patience and skill, turning my scribbles into images, and producing a layout I love.

Thanks also to my daughter, Nicki, my friend Sally, and my clients, for all their support and encouragement.

And, thanks to the collective consciousness and all the thinkers, speakers and writers who have taught me and inspired me.